The Complete
Gammon Cookbook

SIMON &
SCHUSTER

LONDON • NEW YORK • SYDNEY • TORONTO

First published in Great Britain by Simon & Schuster UK Ltd, 2006
A CBS Company

Copyright © Simon and Schuster UK Ltd. All rights reserved

Simon & Schuster UK Ltd
Africa House
64-78 Kingsway
London
WC2B 6AH

1 3 5 7 9 10 8 6 4 2

Additional recipes by Kim Morphew
Design: Jane Norman
Food photography: Gareth Morgans
Stylist and home economist: Kim Morphew
Editor: Emma Marriott

Printed and bound in China

ISBN 0 7432 9541 2

Contents

Foreword

I can't think of a better way to celebrate quality British ingredients than with a book dedicated to British gammon. It's a food that we know how to produce really well in this country, with a delicious full flavour that makes for an exciting dish.

As a boy, I have vivid memories of special family feasts and traditional Christmas dinners featuring impressive glazed gammon joints. The smell and sight of a just-roasted joint was irresistible to me and was always a favourite with the family.

Nonetheless, while traditional joints and the classic 'gammon and pineapple' will always have a place in my heart, there are so many more ways to enjoy this truly versatile meat. It can make a great starter or salad, and can provide a quick and easy family supper or the perfect winter-warmer.

And the gammon revolution has also reached restaurants and pubs around the UK, where chefs are creating innovative, exciting new dishes, and British gammon is a must-have on menus. Many of these well-known eateries and chefs have kindly passed on some of their favourite gammon recipes for inclusion in this book.

So, whether you are a novice or experienced cook, you're sure to be as inspired by this new collection of fabulous, contemporary recipes as I have been. I can guarantee that this modern approach to gammon will have you thinking about this delicious meat in a whole new light. So, all that's left to do is for you to decide which recipe to try first!

Phil Vickery

Introduction

Gammon is a cut of cured bacon, with a full and succulent taste that really satisfies. It works well as a key ingredient in a surprisingly large range of dishes, and it's really simple to prepare and cook.

As gammon is a cured meat, it is treated with salt and, in the past, gammon recipes often involved long-winded methods of soaking to remove the salt. But modern-day curing processes have reduced the amount of salt added so that British gammon no longer requires lengthy soaking prior to its use. For added depth of flavour, gammon is sometimes smoked over smouldering chips of oak, beech, apple, hickory or other woods.

Of course, the true key to success in getting gammon right is using good quality ingredients, so always look for the British Quality Standard Mark or the Little Red Tractor. Gammon that carries this mark comes from farmers committed to high standards of animal welfare, quality control and traceability. The production chain is independently audited to ensure compliance with these standards. So, whether you buy from your local supermarket or butcher, make sure it is British!

The most popular cuts of gammon are unsmoked or smoked gammon joints or steaks. But do look out for other cured joints of gammon, such as honey or dry-cured, that add a delicious flavour to any dish. The ideal cut is middle gammon (also called prime), which is a lean meat available boned and rolled. As a general guide, when buying a gammon joint, allow 150–175 g (5–6 oz) per person.

Keep your gammon in the fridge in its original wrapping below and away from cooked or ready-to-eat food. Gammon is usually vacuum-packed and can be stored in the fridge until the use-by date or frozen on the day of purchase for up to 3 months. Once opened, gammon should be used within 3 days. To defrost, remove it from the original packaging, place it on a

...the true key to success in getting gammon right is using good quality ingredients, so always look for the British Quality Standard Mark or the Little Red Tractor.

plate and cover. Defrost thoroughly in the bottom of the fridge before cooking. Never re-freeze raw meat that has been frozen and then thawed.

Cooking tips for gammon

- Some recipes involve first boiling the gammon joint in water for 10 minutes. This is an integral part of the recipe where the cooking liquor is used and helps remove any salt.

- When boiling a gammon joint, remember it needs a cooking time of approximately 20 minutes per 500 g (1 lb), plus 20 minutes. If the joint is to be roasted and glazed, leave the joint to cool a little after boiling so it can be handled. Then, carefully cut away the skin, leaving a thin layer of fat. Score the fat in a criss-cross or diamond pattern, then glaze and roast in the oven.

- If grilling or frying gammon steaks, cut away and remove the rind with a pair of sharp scissors. Then, to prevent the steak from curling up, snip the outer layers of fat at 1 cm (½-inch) intervals.

- Many of the recipes recommend using a griddle for cooking gammon steaks. If you don't have a griddle pan, use a non-stick frying pan or place them under a preheated grill for the same amount of time.

- Remember not to overcook your gammon as it will end up dry and tough.

- To roast a gammon joint, calculate the cooking time by 20 minutes per 500 g (1 lb) at 180°C/350°F/Gas Mark 4.

Soups and Starters

Gammon and Leek Tortilla

This makes a great snack or canapé to share with friends. Or, for a light lunch, cut the tortilla into quarters and serve with salad and crusty bread.

1. Preheat the oven to Gas Mark 6/200°C/400°F and line a 20 cm (8-inch) loose-bottom or springform cake tin with tin foil, pressing down well against the sides and base. Lightly grease with a little melted butter. Bring a pan of water to the boil and add the potatoes. Cook for 5 minutes. Drain and set aside.

2. Heat the oil in a non-stick frying pan and fry the leeks for 2–3 minutes, until softened. Remove and spoon into the cake tin. Add the gammon and cook over a high heat for a further 5 minutes, until starting to brown.

3. Beat together the eggs, milk and seasoning. Layer the potatoes, leeks and gammon in the cake tin and pour over the egg mixture. Sprinkle over the grated cheese and cook in the oven for 20–25 minutes, until just set and lightly golden.

4. Allow to cool slightly, then turn out of the tin. Cut into 12 bite-size chunks and serve.

Makes 12 squares
Preparation time: 10 minutes
Cooking time: 40 minutes

250 g (8 oz) potatoes, peeled and diced
1 tablespoon olive oil, plus a little extra for greasing
2 leeks, trimmed and sliced thinly
225 g (7½ oz) packet of smoked British gammon steak, fat and rind removed, diced
4 medium eggs, beaten
3 tablespoons milk
50 g (2 oz) Cheddar cheese, grated
seasoning

Serves 4
Preparation time: 15 minutes
Cooking time: 1 hour 25 minutes

750 g (1½ lb) unsmoked British
   gammon joint
500 ml (18 fl oz) dry cider
3 carrots, 2 cut into large chunks
2 leeks, 1 cut into large chunks
1 onion, quartered
8 baby fennel, tops trimmed and reserved
a small handful of fresh flat-leaf parsley,
   stalks separated from leaves, leaves
   chopped
a few sprigs of fresh thyme
225 g (8 oz) bag of baby spinach
freshly ground black pepper

For the dumplings
75 g (3 oz) self-raising flour
40 g (1½ oz) suet
½ teaspoon mustard powder
50 g (2 oz) strong Cheddar, grated finely
a pinch of salt (optional)

St Johns, North London

Poached Gammon and Vegetable Broth with Cheddar Dumplings

This wholesome, hearty soup is delicious served with a generous dollop of wholegrain mustard.

1. Put the gammon in a large pan of water. Bring to the boil and simmer for 10 minutes. Drain and return the gammon to the pan.

2. Add the cider, carrot and leek chunks, onion, fennel trimmings, parsley stalks and thyme. Cover with cold water and bring to the boil. Reduce the heat, cover with a lid and simmer for 45 minutes, skimming the surface often and topping up with water when necessary.

3. Carefully remove the gammon and wrap it in foil. Remove and discard the vegetables with a slotted spoon and strain the liquid through a fine sieve into a jug. You need to have at least 1.2 litres (2 pints) of cooking liquor. (If necessary, top up with hot vegetable stock or rapidly boil to reduce.) Season with black pepper. Thickly slice the remaining leek and carrot.

4. Bring the cooking liquor back to the boil. Meanwhile, mix all the dumpling ingredients in a bowl with the chopped parsley leaves. Add 3–4 tablespoons of cold water to form a soft dough (not too wet). Roll into 4 small balls.

5. Reduce the heat of the liquor to a simmer, add the dumplings and simmer for 10 minutes. Then add the baby fennel, sliced carrots and leeks. Cover and cook for a further 20 minutes, until the vegetables and dumplings are cooked.

6. Just before the end of cooking, remove the rind and excess fat from the gammon and slice thickly. In deep bowls, place a few slices in each, and top with a spoonful of vegetables and a dumpling. Stir the spinach into the cooking liquid to wilt, then ladle the spinach and liquor into the bowls.

Mini Gammon and Horseradish Bites

Scrumptious hot or cold! Wow your guests with these tiny, irresistible Yorkshire puddings filled with gammon. Or cheat and use ready-made, frozen Yorkshire puddings. Just heat according to the packet instructions and divide the cooked gammon into the middle of each one.

1. Preheat the oven to Gas Mark 6/200°C/400°F. Put the flour and salt in a bowl, make a well in the centre and pour in the egg. Whisk gently, combining in the flour. Then gradually add the milk, until a smooth batter.

2. Whiz the gammon in a food processor (or chop very finely with a knife), until minced. Melt the butter in a frying pan and add the gammon. Fry for 5 minutes, stirring with a wooden spoon, until golden all over. Leave to cool.

3. Brush a 12-hole mini muffin tin with the olive oil and put it in the oven for a few minutes to warm. Stir a quarter of the cooked gammon into the batter. Remove the muffin tin from the oven and spoon about 1 tablespoon of the batter into each mini muffin hole until all the batter is used up. Cook in the oven on the highest shelf for 15 minutes, until risen and golden.

4. Meanwhile, mix together the horseradish and crème fraîche, and chill until needed.

5. Transfer the gammon bites to a wire rack and leave to cool. When cold, put a little of the remaining cooked gammon on top of each bite, in the dent where they have sunk. Top with a dollop of horseradish sauce and garnish with chives. Serve immediately, with the sauce in an accompanying dish.

6. To serve hot, reheat the gammon bites in a preheated oven at Gas Mark 7/220°C/425°F for 10 minutes. Garnish and serve as above.

Makes 12
Preparation time: 15 minutes
Cooking time: 20 minutes

50 g (2 oz) plain flour
a pinch of salt (optional)
1 egg, beaten lightly
6 tablespoons full-fat milk
225 g (7½ oz) packet of smoked British gammon steak, fat and rind removed, chopped roughly
15 g (½ oz) unsalted butter
1 tablespoon olive oil
1–2 tablespoons hot horseradish sauce
4 tablespoons crème fraîche
snipped fresh chives, to garnish

Serves 6–8

Preparation time: 10 minutes
  + 6 hours chilling

Cooking time: 30 minutes

375 g (12 oz) honey-cured British
  gammon joint

4 tablespoons brandy

2 small shallots, halved

5 peppercorns

15 g (½ oz) dried wild mushrooms

75 g (3 oz) unsalted butter

2 tablespoons double cream

¼ teaspoon ground allspice

1 tablespoon chopped fresh thyme leaves

caramelised red onion chutney and
  toasted ciabatta, to serve

a few thyme sprigs, to garnish

Gammon and Wild Mushroom Pâté

This pâté is easy to make and perfect served with toasted ciabatta slices
and caramelised red onion chutney.

1. Trim away the rind and excess fat from the gammon, cut into small
   cubes and put into a pan with 3 tablespoons of the brandy, the shallots
   and peppercorns. Cover with water and bring to the boil. Simmer for 30
   minutes, skimming the surface occasionally. Leave to go cold.

2. Meanwhile, soak the mushrooms in boiling water for 15 minutes, drain
   and then chop finely. Set aside.

3. Strain the gammon and reserve the cooking liquor. Put the gammon
   into a food processor and whiz for about 30 seconds. Continue whizzing
   and gradually add 3 tablespoons of the reserved cooking liquor, until
   nearly smooth.

4. Continue whizzing and add the butter, cream, allspice, thyme and remaining
   brandy. Remove from the food processor and spoon into a bowl. Mix in
   the mushrooms, and spoon into 6 x 100 ml (3½ fl oz) ramekins.

5. Chill for 4–6 hours, garnish with thyme sprigs and then serve with
   caramelised red onion chutney and toasted ciabatta.

Chilli Gammon Skewers with Satay Sauce

East meets West with these spicy skewers and satay dipping sauce. They are great for party food, ideal for sharing with friends or as a satisfying light lunch for four, served with a crispy green salad.

1. For the marinade, mix together in a bowl half the coconut milk, 3 tablespoons of the chilli sauce, the olive oil, coriander and lime juice. Cut the gammon steaks into thin 1 cm (½-inch) strips and add to the marinade, turning to coat. Leave for 15 minutes.

2. Meanwhile, for the satay sauce, put the peanut butter, soy sauce, lime zest and remaining chilli sauce into a bowl. Heat the remaining coconut milk in a pan, bring just to the boil and then pour over the peanut butter mix. Stir until combined and then leave to cool.

3. Thread the gammon strips on to 20 small skewers. Lightly brush a griddle pan with some of the olive oil and heat until really hot. Cook the skewers in two batches for 5–6 minutes, turning until golden brown and cooked through. Keep warm and repeat with the remaining skewers. Serve with the satay sauce and lime wedges.

Makes 20
Preparation time: 20 minutes
Cooking time: 12 minutes

200 ml (7 fl oz) coconut milk
4 tablespoons sweet chilli dipping sauce
1 tablespoon olive oil, plus a little extra for griddling
20 g (¾ oz) fresh coriander, chopped finely
2 limes (zest and juice of 1 lime, the other cut into wedges to serve)
450 g (15 oz) packet of smoked British gammon steaks, fat and rind removed
100 g (3½ oz) crunchy peanut butter
1 teaspoon light soy sauce

Gammon and Pea Soup

Serves 4–6
Makes 1.5 litres (2½ pints)
Preparation time: 20 minutes
Cooking time: 15 minutes

25 g (1 oz) butter
450 g (15 oz) packet of smoked British
   gammon steaks, fat and rind removed,
   diced into 1 cm (½-inch) cubes
1 onion, chopped finely
500 g (1 lb) frozen petit pois
1.2 litres (2 pints) fresh chicken stock
300 g (10 oz) can of cannellini beans in
   water, drained and rinsed
freshly ground black pepper

There's nothing better than homemade soup, and this is no exception. Bursting with springtime flavours and chunks of gammon, try adding a dollop of cream when serving. For soup at your fingertips, make double the batch and stock up in the freezer.

1. Melt the butter in a large saucepan and fry the gammon cubes over a medium heat for 5 minutes, until cooked and lightly browned.

2. Remove half the gammon cubes and set aside. Add the onion to the remaining gammon and cook gently for a further 3–4 minutes until softened.

3. Add 400 g (13 oz) of the frozen peas, chicken stock and cannellini beans. Bring to the boil and simmer for 3 minutes. Leave to cool slightly. Meanwhile, put the remaining frozen peas in a bowl, cover with boiling water and set aside until required.

4. In a blender, whiz the soup in batches, until smooth. Return to a clean pan. Drain the reserved peas and add to the soup with the reserved gammon. Gently bring back to the boil, season to taste, and serve.

Light Bites and Salads

Cyrus Todiwala – Café Spice Namasté,
East London

Smoked Gammon Chilli Stir-Fry

The key to success with this dish is having everything prepared and ready to go before cooking. Serve with hot toasted chapattis or pulao rice. For an easy option, use mild curry powder as an alternative to the spice mix.

1. In a bowl, mix together the turmeric, cumin, coriander and water. Set aside. Whiz the tomatoes in a blender until pulped. Set aside.

2. Heat a wok until really hot and add the oil. Reduce to a medium heat and stir-fry the green chillies, ginger, garlic and curry leaves for 2 minutes or until the garlic begins to brown.

3. Add the gammon and continue to stir-fry for 5 minutes, until lightly golden. Stir in the spice mix and cook for 5 minutes, until most of the liquid has evaporated. Stir in the pulped tomato and continue cooking for 3–4 minutes.

4. Increase the heat to high and add the spring onions, green and red peppers and the lime juice. Toss for a couple of minutes, then add the coriander. Check the seasoning and serve with hot toasted chapattis and lime wedges.

Serves 2
Preparation time: 25 minutes
Cooking time: 20 minutes

¼ teaspoon turmeric
½ teaspoon ground cumin
1 teaspoon ground coriander
125 ml (4 fl oz) water
2 large ripe tomatoes, chopped roughly
1 tablespoon groundnut oil
2 green chillies, de-seeded and sliced finely
2 cm (¾-inch) piece of ginger, peeled and grated
2 garlic cloves, sliced
8 curry leaves, sliced finely
450 g (15 oz) packet of smoked British gammon steaks, fat and rind removed, cut into 1 cm (½-inch) slices
3 spring onions, sliced finely
½ green pepper, de-seeded and sliced finely
½ red pepper, de-seeded and sliced finely
Juice of ½ a lime, plus extra wedges to garnish
2 tablespoons chopped fresh coriander
seasoning

Serves 4–6
Preparation time: 30 minutes
Cooking time: 55 minutes

500 g (1 lb) packet of ready-made
  shortcrust pastry
2 tablespoons olive oil
225 g (7½ oz) packet of smoked British
  gammon steak, fat and rind removed,
  diced
5 shallots, quartered
1 tablespoon balsamic vinegar
25 g (1 oz) watercress, chopped roughly
75 g (3 oz) SunBlush tomatoes (or sun-
  dried or cherry tomatoes, chopped finely)
100 g (3½ oz) packet of Somerset goat's
  cheese, sliced thickly
5 tablespoons milk
3 eggs, beaten
freshly ground black pepper

Gammon, Watercress and SunBlush Tomato Tart

This makes a great standby lunch to have in the freezer. Cook the tart, then double-wrap it in greaseproof paper and foil, and freeze for up to 2 months. SunBlush tomatoes are sweet, juicy tomatoes that have been semi-dried in the sun and are available in most supermarkets. If you are short on time, you could cheat and use a ready-made short crust pastry case.

1. Preheat the oven to Gas Mark 5/190°C/375°F and put a baking tray in to heat. Roll out the pastry on non-stick baking paper and use to line a 20 cm x 3 cm (8-inch x 1¼-inch) loose-bottom flan tin. Carefully trim the edges with a knife and chill for 30 minutes.

2. Meanwhile, heat 1 tablespoon of the olive oil in a frying pan and fry the gammon for 5 minutes, until lightly browned and cooked through. Remove and set aside. Heat the remaining oil and gently fry the shallots and balsamic vinegar for 5 minutes until soft. Leave to cool.

3. Prick the base of the pastry case with a fork and line with greaseproof paper. Fill to the top with baking beans or dried pulses. Place on the preheated baking tray and bake for 10 minutes. Remove the paper and beans and bake for a further 5 minutes until cooked.

4. Spoon the shallots over the base, followed by the watercress and gammon. Sprinkle over the SunBlush tomatoes and top with the goat's cheese.

5. Mix together the milk and eggs, season and pour over the tart. Bake in the oven for 25–30 minutes, until set and golden. Serve with a crisp, green salad.

Cat and Mutton, East London

Warm Smoked Gammon and Asparagus Salad

Ideal for Sunday brunch – prepare the gammon in advance, then reheat before serving. Romaine lettuce suits this delicious salad, as does cos, gem or any crisp, green lettuce. For a quicker salad, you could use 4 gammon steaks instead. Simply grill until cooked and then cut into thin strips.

1. Place the gammon in a large saucepan with the remaining gammon ingredients. Cover with cold water and bring to the boil. Reduce the heat, cover and simmer for 1 hour until the meat is cooked. Remove from the heat and leave to cool in the liquor.

2. Meanwhile, blanch the asparagus in boiling water for 2–3 minutes or until tender. Refresh in iced water and cut into 3 cm (1¼-inch) pieces. Place the eggs in cold water, bring to the boil and cook for 90 seconds. Refresh immediately in cold water, peel and cut each in half. Set aside.

3. Mix the shallot, mustard, vinegar and oil together with 1 tablespoon of hot water. When the meat is cool enough to handle, remove and discard the rind and fat. Tear the gammon into chunky pieces and put into a salad bowl.

4. Stir in the dressing and then add the asparagus, parsley and romaine lettuce. Divide between plates and top with the egg halves. Serve with crusty bread.

Serves 4
Preparation time: 25 minutes
Cooking time: 1 hour 5 minutes

750 g (1½ lb) smoked British gammon joint
1 small leek, trimmed and chopped roughly
1 carrot, chopped roughly
1 small onion, quartered
250 ml (8 fl oz) dry white wine
6 black peppercorns
2 bay leaves

For the salad

250 g (8 oz) asparagus spears, trimmed
4 eggs
1 shallot, chopped finely
1 tablespoon wholegrain mustard
1 tablespoon white wine vinegar
2 tablespoons extra virgin olive oil
2 tablespoons chopped fresh parsley
1 romaine lettuce, leaves torn in half

Serves 2
Preparation time: 5 minutes
Cooking time: 30 minutes

450 g (15 oz) packet of British gammon
    steak, fat and rind removed, cut into
    bite-size pieces
1 small onion, chopped finely
432 g (14 oz) can of pineapple chunks in
    juice, drained and juice reserved
1 vegetable stock cube
150 g (5 oz) easy-cook brown rice
900 ml (1½ pints) water
100 g (3½ oz) frozen peas
1 red pepper, de-seeded and sliced
1 tablespoon soy sauce
2 tablespoons chopped fresh chives
freshly ground black pepper

Rosemary Conley CBE
Diet and Fitness Magazine

Gammon with Pineapple Rice

A trendy new twist on gammon with pineapple, there is nothing better
than a risotto. This is a great cheat's version you will love to make time
and time again.

1. Gently dry-fry the gammon and onion in a non-stick pan, stirring for
   3 minutes.

2. Add the pineapple juice, stock cube, rice and water, and bring to the boil.
   Cover with a lid and cook for 25 minutes, stirring occasionally, until the
   rice is tender and most of the liquid is absorbed. (You may need to add
   more boiling water during cooking.)

3. Stir in the pineapple pieces, peas and red pepper, and cook for
   5 minutes. Add the soy sauce and chives, and heat through. Season
   and serve immediately.

Gammon and Artichoke Pizza

A homemade pizza from start to finish that is simply oozing with fresh flavours. And it's irresistible with a glass of chilled dry white wine! If you are short on time, you can use a packet of pizza dough mix or a ready-made pizza base.

1. To make the dough, sift the flour and salt into a bowl. Stir in the yeast and make a well in the centre. Pour the oil and 8 tablespoons of water into the well, and gradually work into the flour, using a wooden spoon to form a soft dough. (If the dough is too dry, add extra water.)

2. Place the dough on to a floured surface and knead well for 5–8 minutes, until smooth and elastic. Return to a clean bowl, cover with lightly oiled cling film and set aside in a warm place for 1 hour, until doubled in size.

3. Meanwhile, preheat the oven to Gas Mark 7/220°C/425°F and place a non-stick baking sheet on the top shelf.

4. For the topping, heat 1 tablespoon of the reserved oil from the artichoke hearts in a frying pan. Add the gammon and fry for 5 minutes, until lightly golden and cooked through. Leave to cool. Stir in the basil and season with black pepper.

5. Place the dough on a floured surface and knead lightly to remove the air. Cut the dough in half and roll each piece into a circle, about 5 mm (¼ inch) thick and 13 cm (5 inches) in diameter. Transfer to the preheated baking sheet. Spread the pesto over the base of each pizza, leaving a 1 cm (½-inch) edge.

6. Top with the artichokes, tomatoes and gammon. Bake in the oven for 15–20 minutes, until the crust is crisp and golden. Scatter with Parmesan shavings, and serve.

Serves 2
Preparation time: 25 minutes
  + 1 hour resting
Cooking time: 25 minutes

For the pizza dough
250 g (8 oz) plain flour
1 teaspoon salt
1 teaspoon easy-blend dried yeast
1 tablespoon olive oil
8–10 tablespoons warm water

For the topping
180 g (6 oz) jar of artichoke hearts marinated in oil (or can of 6 artichoke hearts, quartered), drained and oil reserved
225 g (7½ oz) packet of smoked British gammon steak, fat and rind removed, diced into 1 cm (½-inch) cubes
2 tablespoons chopped fresh basil
freshly ground black pepper
4 tablespoons green pesto
8 cherry tomatoes on the vine, halved
Parmesan shavings, to serve

Serves 4–6
Preparation time: 20 minutes
Cooking time: 10 minutes

4 tablespoons extra virgin olive oil

750 g (1½ lb) honey-cured British gammon joint, fat and rind removed, cut into 1 cm (½-inch) pieces

2 tablespoons sherry vinegar

1 garlic clove, crushed

½ ciabatta (approx. 150 g/5 oz), cut into bite-size chunks

12 yellow or red cherry tomatoes, halved

½ cucumber, quartered and sliced thickly

½ red onion, sliced finely

a handful of fresh basil leaves, torn roughly

1 ripe avocado (optional), stoned, peeled and diced

3 tablespoons toasted pine nuts

freshly ground black pepper

Gammon and Avocado Panzanella Salad

For the best results, use at least one-day-old bread that can really soak up the flavours. This salad can be made up to an hour in advance, although, if you are using avocado, add it at the last minute.

1. Heat 1 tablespoon of the oil in a wide, shallow frying pan and cook the gammon for about 10 minutes, until lightly golden and cooked through. Remove from the heat.

2. Meanwhile, for the dressing, mix together the remaining oil, vinegar and garlic. Pour the dressing into the frying pan, add the ciabatta chunks and toss with the hot gammon. Leave for 5 minutes to cool slightly.

3. Add the remaining ingredients, season well with black pepper, and toss again. Serve.

Midweek Evening Meals

Phil Vickery

Crispy Gammon Strips with Sesame Oil Dressing and Cranberry Salad

This main meal salad with a zingy dressing is a fantastic way to enjoy gammon. For a nutty crunch, add a few toasted walnut halves.

1. For the dressing, place 2 tablespoons of the olive oil in a bowl, add the sesame oil, soy sauce, vinegar and honey, and whisk together. Check the seasoning and adjust if needed. Then mix in the cranberries.

2. Heat a wok or non-stick frying pan until hot, then add the remaining oil. Stir-fry the gammon strips for 8–10 minutes, until lightly browned and crispy.

3. Pour half the dressing over the salad leaves and place on to 2 large plates. Top with the crispy gammon strips and drizzle over the remaining dressing.

Serves 2
Preparation time: 10 minutes
Cooking time: 10 minutes

3 tablespoons olive oil
2 teaspoons sesame oil
2 tablespoons light soy sauce
2½ tablespoons red wine vinegar
1 tablespoon runny honey
50 g (2 oz) dried cranberries
2 x 250 g (8 oz) British gammon steaks, fat and rind removed, cut into 2 cm (¾-inch) strips
120 g (4 oz) bag of mixed salad leaves
seasoning

Vineleaf, St Andrews, Scotland

Baked Gammon Steaks with Creamy Spinach and Gruyère

Serves 4
Preparation time: 20 minutes
Cooking time: 35 minutes

25 g (1 oz) butter

1 onion, chopped finely

350 g (12 oz) bag of baby spinach, washed and dried

a good pinch of freshly grated nutmeg

450 g (15 oz) packet of smoked British gammon steaks

150 ml (¼ pint) whipping cream

1 tablespoon chopped fresh tarragon

1 tablespoon wholegrain mustard

125 g (4 oz) Gruyère cheese, sliced

seasoning

This will soon become a family favourite. For a quick supper, you could prepare the spinach mix in advance, leaving just the gammon to sear and the cream and cheese to add. Delicious!

1. Preheat the oven to Gas Mark 5/190°C/375°F. In a large saucepan, melt the butter over a medium heat, add the onion and gently cook for 3–4 minutes, until softened.

2. Add the spinach, cover with a tight-fitting lid and cook for about 2–3 minutes, stirring from time to time, until just wilted. Stir in the nutmeg and season. Set aside.

3. Heat a griddle pan or non-stick frying pan until really hot. Cut each steak in half and sear for 1 minute on each side. (You may have to do this in batches, depending on the size of your pan.)

4. Put the spinach in a 1.75-litre (3-pint) ovenproof dish and place the steaks on top. Mix the cream, tarragon and mustard together and pour over the steaks.

5. Top the steaks with the sliced Gruyère and bake for 20–25 minutes, until golden brown. Serve with Jersey new potatoes and sliced runner beans.

Brian Turner – Brian Turner Mayfair, London

Gammon Steak with a Mustard and Sage Crust

This crust really jazzes up a gammon steak. To save time, make the crust in advance and chill until needed. If you fancy a change, try using different mustards, like Dijon or wholegrain.

1. Preheat the oven to Gas Mark 7/220°C/425°F. Mix all the crust ingredients together in a bowl. Set aside.

2. Snip the edges of the steaks to prevent the steak curling up. Heat a griddle pan or non-stick frying pan until really hot. Lightly brush both sides of the steaks with the oil and cook each side for 2 minutes to seal. (You may have to do this in batches depending on the size of your pan.)

3. Mix together the mustard and white wine, and brush over one side of the steaks. Press a little of the breadcrumb mix on to the same side, and then sprinkle a little more on top.

4. Put the steaks on to a baking tray and cook in the oven for 20–25 minutes, until the topping is golden. Serve with a mixed salad and potato wedges.

Serves 4
Preparation time: 15 minutes
Cooking time: 30 minutes

For the crust
175 g (6 oz) fresh white breadcrumbs (about 4 slices)
½ onion, grated
2 tablespoons chopped fresh sage
1 tablespoon chopped fresh parsley
1 garlic clove, crushed
50 g (2 oz) butter, softened

For the gammon
2 x 450 g (15 oz) packet of smoked British gammon steaks
2 tablespoons olive oil
1 tablespoon English mustard
1 tablespoon dry white wine

Phil Vickery

Griddled Gammon Steak with Spicy Chickpea Stew

The great thing about this stew is that you can make it as fiery as you like by adding a little extra chilli.

Serves 2
Preparation time: 5 minutes
Cooking time: 20 minutes

2 tablespoons olive oil
1 onion, chopped finely
1 garlic clove, chopped
400 g (13 oz) can of chopped tomatoes
410 g (13 oz) chickpeas in water, drained and rinsed
a pinch of dried red chilli flakes
125 ml (4 fl oz) cold water
1½ tablespoons white wine vinegar
1 tablespoon caster sugar
450 g (15 oz) packet of smoked British gammon steaks
seasoning
chopped fresh parsley, to garnish

1. Heat 1 tablespoon of the olive oil in a saucepan and gently cook the onions and garlic for 3–4 minutes, until softened.

2. Add the chopped tomatoes, chickpeas, chilli flakes, water, vinegar and sugar. Bring to the boil, reduce the heat and simmer for 10 minutes, until thickened. Season well.

3. Meanwhile, heat a griddle pan or non-stick frying pan until hot. Brush the steaks with the remaining oil, and cook on a medium heat for 6–8 minutes, turning until cooked through.

4. Place the gammon steaks in shallow bowls and top with a generous helping of the stew. Garnish with the parsley and serve with fresh green vegetables.

Simpson's-in-the-Strand, London

Gammon Steak and Chips Simpson's Style

It may seem like a luxury using goose fat for these chunky chips but it really does make the perfect chip! Blanch the chips in advance to make dinner time as easy as possible. Serve with fresh green peas for the final touch.

1. Bring a pan of salted water to the boil. Meanwhile, peel and cut the potatoes into thick chips. Plunge the chips into the boiling water and bring back to the boil. Cook for 2 minutes, drain and refresh in cold water. Dry thoroughly with kitchen paper.

2. Reserve 2 tablespoons from the goose fat and set aside. Heat the remaining goose fat over a medium heat and fry the chips in batches, for 8–10 minutes, until golden and cooked. Remove with a slotted spoon and drain on crumpled kitchen paper. Sprinkle with salt and keep warm.

3. Brush both sides of the steaks with the olive oil, and season with the pepper. Heat a griddle pan or grill, until really hot. Cook the steaks for 3–4 minutes on each side, until cooked and lightly browned. (You may have to do this in batches.)

4. Meanwhile, heat the reserved 2 tablespoons of goose fat in a frying pan, until the fat begins to sizzle. Break the eggs into the pan and cook over a medium heat for 4–5 minutes, basting with fat, until the whites are set.

5. To serve, put a gammon steak on a plate with chips, and top each with an egg.

Serves 4
Preparation time: 15 minutes
Cooking time: 20 minutes

750 g (1½ lb) floury potatoes, such as Maris Piper
2 x 340 g (11 oz) can of goose fat
2 tablespoons olive oil
2 x 450 g (15 oz) packet of smoked British gammon steaks
4 large eggs
salt and freshly ground pepper

Calf's Head, Clitheroe, Lancashire

Italian Stuffed Gammon Parcels

Serves 4
Preparation time: 20 minutes
Cooking time: 20 minutes

75 g (3 oz) mozzarella, chopped
50 g (2 oz) sun-dried tomatoes, chopped
4 large fresh basil leaves, shredded
2 x 225 g (7½ oz) packet of smoked
   British gammon steaks, fat and
   rind removed
1 teaspoon olive oil
freshly ground black pepper

A scrumptious dinner, best served with diced, roasted garlic potatoes and green beans. If you are short for time, prepare the gammon parcels up to the end of step three, and chill until needed.

1. Preheat the oven to Gas Mark 5/190°C/375°F. In a bowl, mix together the mozzarella, sun-dried tomatoes and basil. Season with black pepper and set aside.

2. Cut the steaks in half and place each one between two sheets of cling film. Bash with a rolling pin to thin the steaks.

3. Lay each gammon steak on a board and fill the middle with a quarter of the mozzarella mix. Roll up to form a parcel and tie with string.

4. Brush a griddle pan or non-stick frying pan with the oil, and heat until really hot. Sear the gammon parcels on all sides for about 2 minutes, turning every 30 seconds.

5. Transfer the gammon parcels to a small baking dish and pack closely together (this prevents the filling oozing out). Bake for 15–20 minutes until cooked. Serve immediately, with the juices drizzled over and a fresh garden salad and potatoes.

Comfort Food

Anton Edelmann

Bolito Misto of Gammon with Salsa Verde and Olive Oil Mash

This Italian dish literally means 'boiled meat with green sauce'. Try using different types of seasonal vegetables, such as celeriac or parsnips.

1. Put the gammon in a pan with the onions and garlic. Cover with cold water and bring to the boil. Reduce the heat, cover with a lid and simmer for 1¼ hours, skimming often and topping up with more water when necessary.

2. Meanwhile, 30 minutes before the gammon is cooked, make the mash. Put the potatoes and garlic in a pan of water. Bring to the boil and simmer for 20 minutes, until tender. Drain and return to a low heat for 1 minute to dry. Set aside.

3. With a slotted spoon, remove the onion and garlic from the gammon pan and discard. Add the carrots and swede. Bring back to the boil and simmer for 5 minutes. Then add the fennel and leek, and cook for a further 5–8 minutes, until just tender. Remove the vegetables with a slotted spoon and keep warm. Drain the liquor, wrap the gammon in foil and leave to stand for 15 minutes.

4. Mash the potato and garlic. Heat the olive oil and cream in a pan and then gradually stir into the potatoes, until very smooth. Season and keep warm.

5. For the salsa verde, heat the butter in a saucepan and stir in the flour. Cook for 1 minute and then gradually add the stock, mixing well until smooth.

6. Add the cream and horseradish, and simmer for 1 minute until thickened. Pass through a sieve and then add the parsley. Liquidise in a blender, until the sauce is pale green. Season.

7. Remove the fat and rind from the gammon, carve into thin slices and serve with the vegetables, salsa verde and olive oil mash.

Serves 6
Preparation time: 25 minutes
Cooking time: 1½ hours

For the gammon
1.25 kg (3 lb) British smoked gammon joint
3 onions, halved
6 garlic cloves, peeled
3 carrots, cut into 2.5 cm (1-inch) chunks
375 g (12 oz) swede, peeled and cut into 2.5 cm (1-inch) chunks
2 large fennel bulbs, halved and each half cut into thirds
2 large leeks, cut into 5 cm (2-inch) lengths

For the salsa verde
40 g (1½ oz) unsalted butter
2 tablespoons plain flour
300 ml (½ pint) vegetable stock
100 ml (3½ fl oz) double cream
1–2 tablespoons hot horseradish sauce
25g (1 oz) fresh flat-leaf parsley

For the olive oil mash
1.15 kg (2¾ lb) floury potatoes, cut into even cubes
6 garlic cloves, peeled
6 tablespoons olive oil
200 ml (7 fl oz) double cream
seasoning

Serves 4
Preparation time: 10 minutes
Cooking time: 1 hour 5 minutes

300 g (10 oz) split green peas
750 g (1½ lb) smoked British gammon joint
2 bay leaves
12 small shallots, peeled
2 large carrots, cut into 2 cm (¾-inch) chunks
50 g (2 oz) unsalted butter
25 g (1 oz) plain flour
freshly ground black pepper

The Royal Standard of England,
Beaconsfield, Buckinghamshire

Traditional Boiled Gammon with Pease Pudding

This old favourite (like grandma used to make) is simple, tasty and comforting. If you want a real treat, fry the leftover skin to make pork scratchings.

1. Put the split green peas in a large pan and cover with approx. 2.5 cm (1 inch) of water. Bring to the boil, cover with a lid and simmer for about 45 minutes, until tender or you can mash the peas with a fork. (The water may need topping up from time to time.) Place in a sieve over a bowl, and leave to drain off the excess water.

2. Meanwhile, put the gammon and bay leaves in a pan and cover with water. Bring to the boil, reduce the heat and simmer for 30 minutes, skimming the surface during cooking.

3. Add the shallots and carrots, and continue to cook with the gammon for 15 minutes, until the vegetables are just tender. Remove the vegetables with a slotted spoon and keep warm. Then remove the gammon and leave it to cool. Reserve 400 ml (14 fl oz) of the cooking liquor. Place the peas back in the pan, mash with half the butter, and season with black pepper. Keep warm.

4. Melt the remaining butter in a pan, stir in the flour and cook for 1 minute. Then gradually whisk in the reserved cooking liquor until smooth. Bring back to the boil, remove from the heat and keep warm.

5. Remove the rind and excess fat from the gammon and carve into thick slices. Serve with the gravy, vegetables and pease pudding.

The Watermill, St Ives, Cornwall

Gammon Boulangère with Apricot and Cornish Blue Cheese Sauce

'Boulangère' signifies a dish garnished with potatoes, onions and stock. Serve with a glass of West Country ale or cider.

1. Preheat the oven to Gas Mark 4/180°C/350°F, and grease a 1.75-litre (3-pint) ovenproof gratin dish. Put the gammon in a large saucepan, cover with cold water and bring to the boil. Reduce the heat, cover with a lid and simmer for 30 minutes.

2. Meanwhile, put the milk in a large, shallow saucepan with the sliced potatoes. Add enough cold water to cover the potatoes and bring to the boil. Reduce the heat, cover with a lid and simmer for 10 minutes. Drain the potatoes and reserve 75 ml (3 fl oz) of the milk cooking liquid.

3. Melt half the butter in a frying pan and gently fry the onion for 3–4 minutes, until soft. Layer the potatoes and onions in the gratin dish, seasoning each layer, and dot the top with the remaining butter.

4. Remove the gammon from the pan, lay it on top of the potato layers and pour over the hot chicken stock and thyme leaves. Loosely cover with foil and cook in the oven for 30 minutes. Then remove the foil and cook for a further 20–30 minutes, until the meat is tender and the stock has been absorbed. Remove from the oven and cover.

5. To make the sauce, whiz the apricots in a food processor until puréed. In a small pan, slowly heat the cream and cheese, until melted. Stir in the apricot purée and reserved milk cooking liquid, until heated through.

6. Carve the gammon and place it on top of the Boulangère potatoes. Serve with the sauce on the side and fresh green beans.

Serves 6
Preparation time: 25 minutes
Cooking time: 1 hour 40 minutes

1 kg (2 lb) smoked British gammon joint
300 ml (½ pint) skimmed milk
1 kg (2 lb) Maris Piper potatoes, peeled and sliced
50 g (2 oz) butter
1 onion, chopped finely
200 ml (7 fl oz) hot chicken stock
Freshly ground black pepper
1 tablespoon fresh thyme leaves

For the sauce
411 g (14 oz) can of apricot halves in juice, drained
150 ml (¼ pint) double cream
125 g (4 oz) Cornish blue cheese, crumbled

Gammon and Chestnut Mushroom Pie

Golden puff pastry tops a creamy sauce with chunks of gammon and mushrooms. Irresistible with creamy mash and steamed green vegetables.

1. Put the gammon into a large pan, add the wine and cover with water. Bring to the boil and simmer for 15 minutes.

2. Preheat the oven to Gas Mark 5/190°C/375°F and put in a baking tray to warm. Strain the gammon using a slotted spoon and set aside. Pass the cooking liquor through a fine sieve and reserve 200 ml (7 fl oz).

3. In a large pan, melt the butter and gently fry the leeks for 3–4 minutes, until softened. Add the mushrooms and garlic, and continue to cook for 5 minutes.

4. Sprinkle over the flour and stir until everything is coated. Cook for 30 seconds. Then gradually pour in the reserved cooking liquor and cook for 1 minute until thickened, stirring constantly. Season with black pepper.

5. Add the gammon to the leeks and mushrooms, along with the cream, mustard and parsley. Spoon into a deep 1.2-litre (2-pint) pie dish. Unroll the pastry, wet the rim of the dish and place the pastry over the pie. Press down the edges of the pie to seal and use a knife to trim away the excess pastry. (You can use the trimmings to decorate the pie.)

6. Brush the pastry with the beaten egg, place on the preheated baking tray and bake for 35–45 minutes, until golden. Serve with steamed broccoli and carrots.

Serves 4
Preparation time: 20 minutes
Cooking time: 1 hour

1 kg (2 lb) smoked British gammon joint, fat and rind removed, cut into bite-size chunks
300 ml (½ pint) dry white wine
50 g (2 oz) unsalted butter
2 leeks, sliced
250 g (8 oz) chestnut mushrooms, wiped and sliced thickly
1 garlic clove, crushed
3 tablespoons plain flour
5 tablespoons single cream
½ tablespoon wholegrain mustard
3 tablespoons chopped fresh parsley
375 g (12 oz) packet of ready-rolled puff pastry, at room temperature
1 egg, beaten
freshly ground black pepper

Serves 6

**Preparation time: soaking overnight
 + 30 minutes**

Cooking time: 1¾ hours

200 g (7 oz) dried cannellini beans

750g (1 ½ lb) smoked British gammon joint

1 tablespoon olive oil

125 g (4 oz) sliced chorizo sausage

100 g (3 ½ oz) sliced Parma ham, torn
 into pieces

1 onion, chopped

2 garlic cloves, chopped

200 g (7 oz) pork belly, rind removed and
 cut into 1 cm (½-inch) pieces

500 g (1 lb) potatoes, cut into 1 cm
 (½-inch) pieces

2 bay leaves

1.2 litres (2 pints) chicken stock

410 g (14 oz) can of chickpeas, drained
 and rinsed

125 g (4 oz) spring greens, cored and
 shredded finely

Rick's Café, Tooting, London

Caldo Gallego Winter Dish

This traditional Spanish dish is a hearty, soupy stew. Served with crusty bread, it's the perfect winter-warmer. You could use canned cannellini beans instead of the dried version, but add them at the end with the chickpeas.

1. Soak the cannellini beans overnight in a bowl of water and drain. Remove the fat and rind from the gammon and cut into 1 cm (½-inch) pieces.

2. Heat the oil over a low heat in a large saucepan and gently fry the chorizo sausage and Parma ham for a couple of minutes. Add the onion and garlic, and continue to fry for 5 minutes, until softened.

3. Add the gammon, pork belly, cannellini beans, potatoes and bay leaves. Pour in the stock, increase the heat and bring to the boil. Cover with a lid and simmer for 1½ hours, skimming the surface frequently.

4. Stir in the chickpeas and cook for a further 5 minutes. Then add the spring greens, return to a simmer and cook for 2 minutes, until tender.

5. Ladle into shallow bowls and serve with crusty bread.

Woman's Own

Gammon, Stilton and Sage Gnocchi Bake

Serves 4
Preparation time: 15 minutes
Cooking time: 30 minutes

500 g (1 lb) bag of fresh gnocchi

25 g (1 oz) unsalted butter

1 onion, sliced finely

450 g (15 oz) packet of smoked British gammon steaks, fat and rind removed, cut into bite-size chunks

3 sage leaves, chopped finely

2 x 100 g (3 ½ oz) packets of low fat garlic and herb Boursin

150 ml (¼ pint) single cream

25 g (1 oz) mature Stilton

freshly ground black pepper

For the ultimate comfort food, look no further. This gnocchi bake will soon warm up any winter's day. You can use other blue cheeses, like Gorgonzola and, if you can't find fresh sage, substitute with 1 teaspoon of dried sage. Fresh penne or pasta shells also work well in this dish.

1. Preheat the oven to Gas Mark 6/200°C/400°F. Bring a pan of salted water to the boil. Add the gnocchi and cook until they all float to the surface. Drain and set aside.

2. Melt the butter in a wide, deep pan and fry the onion for 3–4 minutes, until softened. Add the gammon and the chopped sage, and cook for a further 5 minutes.

3. Add the garlic and herb cheese and pour in the cream. Stir until the cheese has melted. Season with black pepper.

4. Add the cooked gnocchi and stir to coat. Then spoon into a 1.2-litre (2-pint) ovenproof dish. Sprinkle the Stilton over the top. Bake in the oven for 15–20 minutes, until golden. Serve with rocket salad and garlic bread.

Roasts

Inn on the Green, Cookham Dean, Berkshire

Roast Gammon with Wild Mushrooms and Sauerkraut

This great-tasting sauerkraut will keep for up to two days. Simply reheat when needed. The salt is required when making sauerkraut to remove the water in the cabbage, but is rinsed out before cooking. If you can't get hold of wild mushrooms, use mixed dried mushrooms and rehydrate according to the packet instructions.

1. Season the gammon with the garlic and thyme. Put on to a plate, cover and chill overnight.

2. For the sauerkraut, put the cabbage in a bowl, sprinkle over the sea salt and toss to mix evenly. Leave for 20 minutes, then rinse and dry.

3. Preheat the oven to Gas Mark 4/180°C/350°F. Heat the sunflower oil (1 tablespoon) in a large non-stick pan until hot, and brown the gammon on all sides. Transfer to a roasting tray and cook in the oven for 40–50 minutes, until the meat is cooked through and starting to turn golden brown.

4. Meanwhile, for the sauerkraut, heat the sunflower oil (2 tablespoons) in a large saucepan. Add the onion and cook for 3–4 minutes, until softened. Grate the apple and add to the onion, followed by the cabbage, and cook for 1–2 minutes. Then add the caraway seeds, cider and vinegar. Cover with a lid and cook for 20–25 minutes, stirring from time to time, until tender.

5. Remove the gammon from the roasting pan, cover with foil and leave to rest for 15 minutes. Add the Madeira wine to the roasting tray and simmer on the hob for a few minutes. Pass through a sieve and keep warm.

6. Meanwhile, for the mushrooms, melt the butter in a pan and fry the shallots for 2 minutes, until softened. Add the mushrooms and cook for another 5 minutes. Stir in the parsley and season.

7. Carve slices of the gammon and serve with the sauerkraut and mushrooms, drizzled with the Madeira pan juices.

Serves 6

Preparation time: chilling overnight + 30 minutes

Cooking time: 1 hour

For the gammon
1 kg (2 lb) smoked British gammon joint
3 garlic cloves, crushed
2 tablespoons fresh thyme leaves
1 tablespoon sunflower oil
175 ml (6 fl oz) Madeira wine

For the sauerkraut
500 g (1 lb) white cabbage, cored and shredded finely
2 tablespoons sea salt
2 tablespoons sunflower oil
1 small onion, quartered and sliced thinly
3 eating apples, peeled and cored
1 teaspoon caraway seeds
200 ml (7 fl oz) dry cider
2 tablespoons cider vinegar

For the wild mushrooms
50 g (2 oz) butter
4 large shallots, chopped finely
500 g (1 lb) mixed wild mushrooms, wiped and trimmed
2 tablespoons chopped fresh parsley
seasoning

Serves 4–6
Preparation time: 30 minutes
Cooking time: 2 hours 35 minutes

2 kg (4½ lb) unsmoked British
   gammon joint
1 onion, halved
25–35 cloves
2 bay leaves
2 celery sticks, cut into 2.5 cm (1-inch)
   pieces
125 ml (4 fl oz) water
125 g (4 oz) caster sugar
10 kumquats (or 2 medium oranges),
   sliced with skin on, ends discarded
2 tablespoons runny honey
175 g (6 oz) soft brown sugar

For the sauce
2 tablespoons redcurrant jelly
300 ml (½ pint) red wine
juice of 2 oranges
6 kumquats (or 1 medium orange), sliced
   with skin on, ends discarded
100 g (3½ oz) cold butter, diced

The Ship Inn, Elie, Fife, Scotland

Kumquat and Honey-glazed Gammon

This sticky, glazed gammon is a twist on the all-time Christmas favourite.
It also makes a delicious Sunday roast. If you can't get hold of kumquats,
substitute with orange slices and follow the same cooking instructions.

1. Put the gammon in a pan with the onion, 4 of the cloves, the bay leaves and
   celery. Top with cold water and bring to the boil. Cover with a lid and simmer
   for 2 hours. Remove the gammon, discard the liquid and leave to cool.

2. Meanwhile, preheat the oven to Gas Mark 6/200°C/400°F. Put the water
   and caster sugar into a saucepan. Heat gently to dissolve the sugar, then
   bring to the boil. Add the kumquats and simmer for 2–3 minutes, until
   soft. Drain and leave the kumquats to cool. Reserve the syrup.

3. When the gammon is cool, cut away the rind and fat until a thin layer of
   fat remains. Score the remaining fat with a knife.

4. Line a roasting tin with foil and place the gammon on top. Brush the
   honey over the gammon and pack the soft brown sugar around it with
   your hands. With the remaining cloves, pierce one into each sliced,
   cooled kumquat and stick into the gammon fat. Pull up the tin foil to
   protect the exposed areas of meat.

5. Cook the gammon in the oven for 30–40 minutes, basting with the
   collected juices in the foil every 10 minutes, until caramelised and brown
   in colour. Leave to stand for 10 minutes.

6. Meanwhile, make the sauce. Put the reserved sugar syrup, redcurrant
   jelly, red wine and orange juice into a pan and bring to the boil. Simmer
   for 15 minutes, until reduced by half. Add the kumquat slices and simmer
   for 2–3 minutes, until soft. Whisk in the butter, a little at a time, until
   melted and the sauce begins to thicken. Keep warm.

7. Carve the gammon into slices and serve with the sauce and new potatoes.

Cherry-glazed Earl Grey Gammon

A special dish and a wonderful way to cook gammon. The Earl Grey tea infuses into the meat and the sweet, red fruits complement the salty gammon. If you can't find red fruit iced tea, brew any red berry fruit tea in 1.5 litres (2½ pints) of boiling water. Leave to go cold before using.

1. Put the gammon and Earl Grey tea in a large pan. Pour over the red fruit iced tea and top up with cold water to cover the gammon. Bring to the boil, cover with a lid and simmer for 1 hour. Leave to cool in the liquor.

2. Preheat the oven to Gas Mark 7/220°C / 425°F. Mix the jam with 2 tablespoons of the cooled liquor and then pass the jam mixture through a sieve until it is smooth. Put the jam mixture into a pan and bring to the boil. Simmer for 3–4 minutes, until thickened.

3. Remove the rind from the gammon, leaving a thin layer of fat, and score with a sharp knife. Spread the cherry glaze over the fat, reserving a little for later.

4. Line a roasting tin with foil, add the gammon, and cook in the oven for 20 minutes, until caramel brown in colour. Brush over the rest of the glaze and leave to stand for 10 minutes. Then carve and serve with mange tout and roast potatoes, or leave to go cold before serving.

Serves 4
Preparation time: 10 minutes
Cooking time: 1 hour 25 minutes

1 x 1.2 kg (3 lb) unsmoked British gammon joint
3 tablespoons Earl Grey tea leaves
1.5 litres (2 ½ pints) red fruit iced tea
5 tablespoons red cherry jam

Serves 6
Preparation time: 15 minutes
Cooking time: 1¾ hours

2 kg (4½ lb) unsmoked British
   gammon joint
1 litre (1¾ pints) apple juice
500 ml (18 fl oz) dry cider
1 cinnamon stick
3 tablespoons balsamic glaze
1 kg (2 lb) cooking apples, peeled, cored
   and cut into 1 cm (½-inch) pieces

Sticky Balsamic Roasted Gammon with Apple Sauce

This tangy, glazed gammon with a fruity edge is really delicious served with crispy roast parsnips and spuds. Balsamic glaze is available from most supermarkets or you can rapidly boil balsamic vinegar in a pan, until thick and syrupy.

1. Put the gammon in a pan, pour over the apple juice and cider, and add the cinnamon stick. If necessary, top up with water to cover. Bring to the boil, cover with a lid and simmer for 1½ hours.

2. Preheat the oven to Gas Mark 7/220°C/425°F. Drain and reserve the gammon cooking liquor. Remove and discard the gammon skin, leaving a thin layer of fat. Score the fat with a sharp knife.

3. Put the gammon on a foil-lined baking tray and brush 1 tablespoon of the balsamic glaze over the fat. Roast in the oven for 10–15 minutes, until sticky and caramel brown.

4. Meanwhile, put the apples in a pan with the remaining balsamic glaze and 5 tablespoons of the cooking liquor. Cover with a lid and cook over a gentle heat for about 5 minutes or until the apples are soft, stirring from time to time to prevent sticking.

5. Leave the gammon to stand for 10 minutes, then slice thickly and serve with the apple sauce, roast potatoes, parsnips and peas.

Braised Gammon with Butter Beans

A hearty dish that is full of flavour. You can always replace the butter beans with other pulses, like pinto or cannellini.

1. Preheat the oven to Gas Mark 6/200°C/400°F. On the hob, heat the oil in a flame and ovenproof casserole dish. Add the onion, carrots, celery, swede and rosemary and gently fry for 5 minutes, until they are beginning to soften.

2. Add the butter beans, chopped tomatoes, wine and water. Then add the gammon, fat side up, and bring to the boil.

3. Cover with a lid and transfer to the oven. Cook for 50 minutes. Then remove the lid and cook for a further 20 minutes, until the fat is golden brown and slightly crispy.

4. Remove the gammon from the casserole dish and carve thick slices. Serve with fresh green vegetables.

Serves 4–6
Preparation time: 20 minutes
Cooking time: 1 hour 20 minutes

2 tablespoons olive oil
1 onion, chopped finely
2 carrots, sliced thickly
2 sticks of celery, sliced thickly
300 g (10 oz) swede, peeled and diced
1 tablespoon chopped fresh rosemary
2 x 420 g (14 oz) can of butter beans, drained and rinsed
400 g (13 oz) can of chopped tomatoes
250 ml (8 fl oz) dry white wine
300 ml (½ pint) water
1.2 kg (3 lb) smoked British gammon joint, rind removed and fat scored with a sharp knife

Serves 6

Preparation time: 15 minutes + 24 hours chilling

Cooking time: 1 hour

1.2 kg (3 lb) unsmoked British gammon joint

15 g (½ oz) fresh flat-leaf parsley

15 g (½ oz) fresh coriander

15 g (½ oz) fresh chives

15 g (½ oz) fresh thyme, leaves removed if stems are woody

1 tablespoon English mustard

Herby Gammon

This juicy, succulent gammon joint with a herby coating is perfect for buffets and sandwiches, or simply on its own with a crisp salad.

1. Put the gammon in a pan and cover with water. Bring to the boil and simmer for 1 hour, skimming the surface and topping up with more water when necessary. Drain and set aside to cool a little.

2. Meanwhile, put the herbs in a food processor and whiz until finely chopped. Transfer to a plate.

3. When the gammon is cool enough to handle, remove the skin and rind. Then brush mustard all over the gammon.

4. Roll the gammon in the herbs, ensuring that it is fully covered. Wrap it tightly with a double layer of foil, and chill for 24 hours.

5. To serve, remove the cling film and slice finely. Serve with potato salad.

Addresses

St Johns

Poached Gammon and
Vegetable Broth with
Cheddar Dumplings

91 Junction Road
London
N19 5QU

Tel: 0207 272 1587

Café Spice Namasté

Cyrus Todiwala's Smoked
Gammon Chilli Stir-Fry

16 Prescot Street
London E1 8AZ

Tel: 0207 488 9242
Fax: 0207 488 9339
www.cafespice.co.uk

Cat and Mutton

Warm Smoked Gammon
and Asparagus Salad

76 Broadway Market
London
E8 4QJ

Tel: 0207 254 5599

Vineleaf Restaurant

Baked Gammon Steaks with
Creamy Spinach and Gruyère

131 South Street
St Andrews
Fife
KY16 9UN

Tel: 01334 477497
Email: vineleaf@tesco.net
www.vineleafstandrews.co.uk

Millennium Hotel

Gammon Steak with a
Mustard and Sage Crust

Brian Turner Mayfair
Millennium Hotel London Mayfair
Grosvenor Square
London
W1K 2HP

Tel: 020 7596 3444

Simpson's-in-the-Strand

Gammon Steak and Chips
Simpson's Style

100 Strand
London
WC2R 0EW

Tel: 0207 836 9112

Calf's Head

Italian Stuffed
Gammon Parcels

Worston
Clitheroe
BB7 1QA

01200 441218

The Royal Standard of England

Traditional Boiled Gammon
with Pease Pudding

Brindle Lane
Forty Green
BeaconsField
Bucks
HP9 1XT

Tel: 01494 673382

The Watermill

Gammon Boulangère with
Apricot and Cornish Blue
Cheese Sauce

Lelant Downs
Nr St Ives
Cornwall
TR27 6LQ

Tel: 01736 757912
Email: watermill@btconnect.com
www.thewatermillincornwall.co.uk

Rick's Café

Caldo Gallego Winter Dish

122 Mitcham Road
Tooting
SW17 9NH

Tel: 020 8767 5219

The Inn on the Green

Roast Gammon with Wild
Mushrooms and Sauerkraut

The Old Cricket Common
Cookham Dean
Berkshire
SL6 9NZ

Tel: 01628 482638
www.theinnonthegreen.com

The Ship Inn

Kumquat and
Honey-glazed Gammon

The Toft
Elie
Fife
Scotland
KY9 1DT

Tel: 01333 330246
Fax: 01333 330864
Email: info@ship-elie.com
www.ship-elie.com

Index